SUPERSONIC JETS

BY DENNY VON FINN

150

160

170

BELLWETHER MEDIA • MINNEAPOLIS, MN

TM

Are you ready to take it to the extreme?
Torque books thrust you into the action-packed world
of sports, vehicles, and adventure. These books may
include dirt, smoke, fire, and dangerous stunts.
WARNING: read at your own risk.

This edition first published in 2010 by Bellwether Media, Inc.

No part of this publication may be reproduced in whole or in part without written permission of the publisher.
For information regarding permission, write to Bellwether Media, Inc., Attention: Permissions Department,
5357 Penn Avenue South, Minneapolis, MN, 55419.

Library of Congress Cataloging-in-Publication Data

Von Finn, Denny.
  Supersonic jets / by Denny Von Finn.
    p. cm. – (Torque. The world's fastest)
  Includes bibliographical references and index.
  Summary: "Amazing photography accompanies engaging information about supersonic jets.
The combination of high-interest subject matter and light text is intended for students in grades 3 through 7"
–Provided by publisher.
  ISBN 978-1-60014-287-1 (hardcover : alk. paper)
  1. High-speed aeronautics--Juvenile literature. 2. Supersonic planes--Juvenile literature. I. Title.
TL571.V66 2010
629.133'349--dc22
                                    2009013254

Printed in the United States of America.

CONTENTS

What Are Supersonic Jets?

Supersonic jets are the world's fastest aircraft. "Supersonic" means they travel faster than sound. The speed of sound changes with **altitude** and air temperature. It is 761 miles (1,225 kilometers) per hour at **sea level** and 59 degrees Fahrenheit (15 degrees Celsius). The point at which jets reach supersonic speed is called the **sound barrier**.

Sound travels 5,280 feet (1,600 meters) per second. The speed of sound is also called **Mach 1**. Supersonic jets exceed Mach 1. The SR-71 Blackbird holds the record for the fastest manned jet aircraft. In 1976, it recorded a speed of Mach 3.3. That's 2,193 miles (3,529 kilometers) per hour. That is more than three times the speed of sound!

American pilot George Welch was the first person to fly a supersonic jet. In 1953, he reached Mach 1.1 in a YF-100 Super Sabre.

The YF-100 Super Sabre and the SR-71 Blackbird were **military aircraft**. Only two **passenger aircraft** have reached supersonic speeds. The Tu-144 and the Concorde made their first supersonic flights in 1969.

Supersonic Jet Technology

A supersonic aircraft is powered by jet engines. Fans pull air into the engines. Fans inside the engines **compress** the air. The air then mixes with burning fuel. The hot air expands and rushes out the back of the engines. This creates **thrust**. The thrust pushes the aircraft forward with great force.

Fast Fact

Some of the air pulled into a jet engine is used to cool the engine so that it does not melt!

11

Fast Fact

"Shock collars" are clouds of water vapor that often occur when jets travel at supersonic speeds.

Supersonic jets travel faster than the sound they create. The jet pushes the **sound waves** into the shape of a cone. These waves are just like the waves created by a fast boat. The sound waves make a loud crack when they pass overhead. This noise is called a **sonic boom**.

A supersonic jet has a long, skinny **fuselage**. This thin shape decreases **friction** and **drag**. Friction and drag slow down an aircraft. Supersonic jets must withstand high temperatures created by friction. Their fuselage and wings are often made of a strong material like **titanium**.

The Future of Supersonic Jets

Future supersonic jets will allow travelers to go anywhere in the world in just a few hours. The A2 is a concept aircraft. That means it is just an idea. This jet would carry 300 passengers at 3,400 miles (5,500 kilometers) per hour. Its hydrogen fuel would create no **pollution**.

Smaller supersonic jets are also being developed.
These aircraft are supersonic business jets (SBJs).
They are designed to carry eight to twelve people.
Aerion is one of the top developers of SBJs. Aerion SBJs
are designed to cruise at Mach 1.1 without creating a
sonic boom. They are expected to be available in 2014.

Fast Fact

Some scientists believe that future hypersonic jets will be able to travel Mach 15!

Some future jets will be even faster than supersonic. These aircraft are called "hypersonic." Hypersonic means faster than Mach 5.

The Boeing X-43 is an unmanned experimental jet. In 2004, it traveled 7,546 miles (12,100 kilometers) per hour. That's nearly 10 times the speed of sound!

GLOSSARY

altitude—the measure of an object's height above sea level

compress—to squeeze

drag—a force that reduces speed

friction—a force created when two objects rub against each other; supersonic jets create friction with the air they speed through.

fuselage—the main body of an aircraft

Mach 1—the speed of sound, named for scientist Ernst Mach

military aircraft—aircraft used by the military

passenger aircraft—aircraft used by the public

pollution—harmful particles released into the environment

sea level—the average level of the ocean; sea level is used to measure the height of any object or place.

sonic boom—the loud noise created when something surpasses the speed of sound

sound barrier—the point at which an aircraft reaches supersonic speed

sound waves—vibrations that can be heard; the sound waves from a supersonic jet travel through the air.

thrust—the force that moves an aircraft

titanium—a lightweight metal that is combined with other metals; titanium is used to build aircraft.

TO LEARN MORE

AT THE LIBRARY

Amato, William. *Supersonic Jets*. New York, N.Y.: PowerKids Press, 2004.

David, Jack. *F-16 Fighting Falcons*. Minneapolis, Minn.: Bellwether Media, 2007.

Zobel, Derek. *United States Air Force*. Minneapolis, Minn.: Bellwether Media, 2009.

ON THE WEB

Learning more about supersonic jets is as easy as 1, 2, 3.

1. Go to www.factsurfer.com.

2. Enter "supersonic jets" into the search box.

3. Click the "Surf" button and you will see a list of related Web sites.

With factsurfer.com, finding more information is just a click away.

INDEX